ON THE TRACKS

MOTORCYCLE MANIA

David and Patricia Armentrout

Rourke
Publishing LLC
Vero Beach, Florida 32964

www.rourkepublishing.com

PHOTO CREDITS: Cover ©Harry Starr; title page ©afaizal; pp. 4, 5 ©Daimler Chrysler Media; pp. 6 ©Courtesy of Library of Congress; pp. 7 ©Tan Kian Khoon; pp. 9 ©Mike Patrick; pp. 10 ©William Mahar; pp. 12 ©Yamaha; pp. 13 ©Pascal Janssen; pp. 14, 15 ©Keith Robinson; pp. 16, 20 ©Honda Media; pp. 17 ©BMW Media; pp. 18, 19 ©Kawasaki; pp. 21 ©Daniel Gustavsson; pp. 22 ©JustASC.

Title page: *Racers hug the curve on a motorcycle circuit track.*

Editor: Robert Stengard-Olliges

Cover design by Nicola Stratford

Library of Congress Cataloging-in-Publication Data

Armentrout, David, 1962-
 On the tracks / David and Patricia Armentrout.
   p. cm. -- (Motorcycle mania II)
 ISBN-13: 978-1-60044-590-3
 1. Motorcycle racing--Juvenile literature. 2. Motorcycles--History--Juvenile literature. I.
Armentrout, Patricia, 1960- II. Title.
 GV1060.A744 2008
 796.7'5--dc22
                             2007016379

Printed in the USA

CG/CG

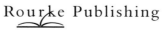

Rour͜ke Publishing

www.rourkepublishing.com – rourke@rourkepublishing.com
Post Office Box 3328, Vero Beach, FL 32964

TABLE OF CONTENTS

THE FIRST MOTORCYCLE

Gottlieb Daimler, a German engineer, built the first two wheeled, gasoline powered vehicle in 1885. His creation wasn't exactly speedy; it ran about seven miles (11.26km) an hour. However, it didn't take long for Daimler's simple motorcycle to evolve into a reliable and popular **mode** of transportation.

Gottlieb Daimler

Gottlieb Daimler's two wheeled machine.

RACING TRACKS

Daimler had no idea his first motorcycle would lead to a new motor sport. But by the early 1900s, motorcycle racing gained a foothold in Europe and quickly spread around the world. Organized races were held on public roads, horse racetracks, and on wooden tracks called **velodromes**. As technology improved, and motorcycles became faster, motorcycle racetracks became necessary.

An early motorcycle race on a wooden track.

It takes a professional track to safely handle the high speeds of sportbikes and superbikes.

Motorcycle sports are generally broken into two groups, road and off road. Each group has several smaller groups.

IN THE DIRT

Dirt track racing, also known as flat track, is one of the earliest forms of motorcycle racing. Dirt offers good traction and is forgiving in a fall. Tracks range from a quarter mile (.40 km) to a mile (1.6 km) long. Flat track is as exciting to watch as it is to race. Riders race elbow to elbow at breakneck speed on hard packed dirt ovals.

Speedway races are slightly different. Racers use controlled slides to maintain speed on a loose dirt or **shale** surface. Oval tracks range from 250 to 425 meters (820 to 1395 feet) long.

Dirt flies as a speedway racer power slides through the turn.

Flat track TT courses have left and right turns and at least one jump.

Most flat track courses are dirt, but some indoor tracks have a polished concrete surface. Concrete tracks are heated and then sprayed with sticky syrup. Soft rubber tires, hot concrete, and sticky syrup add up to great tire traction.

Ice racing is popular in cold climates.

Ice is another popular motorcycle track surface. Ice racing and ice speedway are two forms of motorcycle ice racing. Races take place on natural ice or on indoor ovals. Depending on the kind of race, riders use either rubber or metal studded tires. Rubber tires slide easily on the frozen surface while studded tires provide grip.

MOTOCROSS TRACKS

Some racing tracks are flat and some definitely are not! The term *motocross* combines the words motorcycle and cross country. Motocross racing tracks are built on grass, dirt, sand, mud, and gravel, and they're not flat. Motocross tracks have plenty of ups and downs, **berms**, dips, and jumps. Racers get airborne as they speed through the hilly courses.

A racer takes advantage of an empty motocross course to fine tune his skills.

Motocross racing on the beach is called Beachcross.

PAVED TRACKS

Motorcycle road racing takes place on **tarmac**, a paved surface. Some road races are held on public roads that are closed temporarily. Road races are quite challenging. Road courses take riders through narrow city streets, twisting country roads, and up and down hills. Races can last for hours, as riders may be required to complete many laps.

Racers make their way through a country neighborhood.

Spectators watch road racing action.

Motorcycle road races are also held on **circuit** tracks. Circuit tracks are built specifically for racing. Some are simple ovals, while others are more like road courses. They can have left and right turns, hairpin turns, a corkscrew turn, or an S-bend turn.

Superbike races are on circuit tracks. Superbikes have soft rubber tires that heat up as they speed along the track. The rubber gets very sticky when hot, and sticky tires grip tarmac best.

Racers navigate left and right turns and elevation changes on this circuit track.

Sticky tires grip the pavement as racers lean into the curves.

ON THE STRIP

Drag bikes can't run laps on a circuit course because they're built for straight line racing. Drag bikes race on a drag strip—a flat, straight, paved course.

An aerodynamic shape reduces wind resistance and improves performance.

Racers "burn rubber" to warm up their tires.

Drag races are about speed, not distance. Races are only a quarter mile (.40 km) or an eighth mile (.20 km) long. A column of lights separates the two lanes at the starting line. Racers keep a keen eye on the lights. A green light means GO, and in less than eight seconds, the race is over!

TRAILS

There are flat tracks, hilly tracks, ice tracks, and sometimes no track at all. Sometimes the best place to ride is on an off road trail. Off road motorcycle trails can be wide open or heavily wooded with tight passages. Off road trails include all kinds of **terrain**, from dirt, sand, and mud, to grass, gravel, and rock.

Off road riders should stay on established trails.

Mud flies on an enduro course.

Enduro events take riders on lengthy off road courses with varied terrain.

NO END TO RACING

Superbikes wouldn't cut it on a dirt oval, and even though drag bikes are super fast, they would be useless on a speedway track.

Tracks and trails evolve just like the motorcycles that race on them. Riders may debate which bike is the fastest, or which track is the most challenging. But most would agree on one thing— as long as there are motorcycles, there will be motorcycle racing.

Riders contemplate a steep hill climb.

GLOSSARY

berms (BERMZ) — banked walls of earth

circuit (SUR kit) — a route that starts and finishes in the same place

mode (mohd) — a way of doing something

shale (shayl) — a rock formed from hard clay or mud

tarmac (TAR mak) — a paving material of tar and stone, or the pavement itself

terrain (tuh RAYN) — the ground or land

velodromes (VEH leh drome) — wooden racetracks built especially for bicycle racing

INDEX

FURTHER READING

Mezzanotte, Jim. *Flat Track*. Gareth Stevens Audio, 2006.
Levy, Janet. *Motocross Races*. Rosen Publishing Group, 2007.
Norman, Tony. *Motorcycle Racing*. Gareth Stevens Audio, 2006.

WEBSITES TO VISIT

www.amadirectlink.com
http://www.flattrack.com
www.msf-usa.org

ABOUT THE AUTHORS

David and Patricia Armentrout specialize in writing nonfiction books for young readers. They have had several books published for primary school reading. The Armentrouts live in Cincinnati, Ohio, with their two children.

J
796.7 Armentrout, David
ARM On the tracks

796.6
WOO
Wood, Tim
Mountain biking

2638

GILL MEMORIAL LIBRARY
Broad & Commerce Sts.
Paulsboro, NJ 08066
856-423-5155